How To Understand The Subconscious Mind

M. L. PILGRIM

TO MY WIFE AND MY SON, THIS BOOK IS FOR YOU.

How To Understand The Subconscious Mind

Table of Contents

Introduction

I want to thank you and congratulate you for downloading the book, *"How To Understand The Subconscious Mind"*.

This book contains proven steps and strategies on how to discover the other side of your mind.

It is known that there are many things that can permeate the human soul, and that can enter into the depths of a person without knowing much information about it, so the process of dealing with the human soul is one of the most difficult things that people can learn about or encounter at any time.

For this reason, we may find that the specializations that can be included in the study of human behavior, or all behaviors that a person performs in his daily life, as well as reactions to all situations that he can face him on any day of his life are among the most difficult disciplines in the world.

Which many great scholars have worked on, who have had the most influential role in knowing all these things and controlling some of them, which a person can perform in his days in which he lives unintentionally. It is really surprising that we can control the actions that we can take at every moment of our lives and our reaction to all things that we can be exposed to no matter what it is to come up with the ideal solution.

Here, we will tell you some small steps and techniques to master your own reactions even the ones that you cannot take full control of.

Thanks again for buying this book, I hope you enjoy it!

Chapter 1
What is the subconscious mind?

Some psychologists talk about the subconscious as a pearl buried within the human psyche that needs someone to discover it. The philosopher Socrates advised us to dive into the depths of our human souls, to recognize ourselves without depending on a theory or law, as we are more aware of ourselves than others ever will.

In order for the concept of the subconscious to be further approximated, it has been likened to two mountains: the first mountain, which is the conscious mind; It is the mind with which a person deals with his external and internal world based on certain principles and foundations in life, and many see it as logical and acceptable, and this conscious mind is formed since childhood. It is formed by a combination of several factors that we come across with time, as methods of education, and the nature of family, also the social, moral, and religious factors. The first mountain starts to rise and grow more than the other mountain, which is the subconscious mind. We will discuss the relation between them in the next chapter.

The definition of the subconscious is the vessel that brings together all the thoughts and feelings that a person has experienced, which one day will go out to the outside world in a certain way to express his personality.

This vessel, if a person enters into it negative thoughts and experiences and feelings of hatred and envy, then the result is a sick and sinister personality, but if he enters positive thoughts, beautiful feelings and wonderful memories full of love, friendliness and tolerance, then the personality that results from this is a positive and successful personality.

The subconscious mind can capture thousands of signals through a person's senses, and begins to store these signs and the accompanying feelings together until they appear again as human tendencies and interests, and the subconscious may have an impact on person's decisions that emanate from him, especially quick decisions.

Methods of connecting with the subconscious

The human subconscious mind usually contains a great deal of wisdom and knowledge, which is not exploited by most of us in the best possible way. We need to unleash this subconscious mind in order to liberate its potential strength and make it a reason for success and change in life, and a person can enter the subconscious by following some advices and methods that may help in this, including:

- *Meditation*

Meditation is the simplest way to reach the subconscious mind; It takes the person to a state close to a dream, the brain's actions become slower and more organized, and the noise of daily life is less effective and much quieter.

In the normal situation of a person, the scope of the work of his brain is in the beta pattern, a condition that is related to wakefulness, and may be accompanied by tension, anger, or anxiety.

But in the case of deep meditation, the pattern is transferred to the delta mode. Where a change results in the quality of human thinking, and the flow of ideas from his subconscious becomes smoother to begin to impose themselves in the state of consciousness.

In this case, the person must allow these ideas to flow, and the more he meditates, the more skilled he becomes in solving a specific situation. He finds solutions to problems or dilemmas he faces, and a person can learn to meditate quickly, because it is not hard and does not need much time.

- *Listening to creativity*

The way the subconscious mind talks with a person is without words. It speaks with pictures, sounds, and music. Listening to the individual's self helps his mind to express itself. For a person who is

practicing a certain type of arts - such as pottery or other – meditation helps him to strongly show a certain aspect of his personality.

- *Following instinct*

If a person tries to confront a problem or make a specific decision about something that happened to him, then the first thing that comes to his mind is the subconscious talk, and the person may think at some point that the first decision to pop up in his mind is not correct; However, these decisions may be incredibly accurate and effective.

Chapter 2
The relationship between conscious and subconscious mind

The human mind is the tool that changed the course of the seas and rivers, moved mountains and plateaus, brought out from the barren desert food and water, made from the sea, land and air a means of transportation, brought the mankind to space, made planes, ships and atomic bombs and discovered many things.

In spite of all these discoveries, the mind is still unknown and confusing to us, and we could not reach how to reach compatibility with the soul through the mind, and how to make from it a means of happiness and peace of mind that everyone searches for in this life, which is predominantly misfortune and materialism.

We must know that every person possesses a higher self, which is conscience and a lower self, which are instincts and desires, and that instincts are the same in all mankind, the instincts are the same but desires and reason are what makes some control their instincts and makes others drift towards it.

We must also know that the conscious mind does not work well if we put into it some of the bad beliefs that you always think about. For example, the fear that we leave it to dominate us makes the conscious mind a bit paralyzed.

Every human being has a conscious mind and subconscious mind which is the "secret storage" of mind, meaning that it stores many events in your long-lasted memory, whether they are positive or negative, and then according to the situation that the person is exposed to, if he has a similar situation, these events suddenly appear before him and his life is interrupted.

The first step in discovering a person's own self and hence reaching happiness is freedom from obsessions, beliefs and old ideas that have arisen and accumulated in the subconscious mind.

For example, if one little girl happens to have experienced a problem within her mother's life, that problem will remain with the subconscious mind of the child. As a result, it is possible that the girl may hate marriage or fear that the same problem will happen to her as it happened to her mother with her husband.

Hence, we need to use a method of psychological treatment and rehabilitation for this girl so that she can move on from a feeling of misery to the happiness stage that every girl dreams about, in order to live a new life with the one she loves and then build a better family with him, so she must go out of the subconscious stage to the awareness stage until she becomes a better version of herself who brings happiness to her family.

Therefore, it is necessary for the father and mother to understand that they are the reason for creating some fears in the lives of children, and they are also those who make them innovate or make them losers and afraid of people and society.

For example, when one of the mothers puts her young son in a dark room alone for a period of time, then from there the child shall grow a fear of darkness, this obsession continues to grow in his subconscious mind until it becomes a knot for him.

Which makes him afraid of darkness, dark places, the subway, and tunnels. He will feel that he is dying or suffocating because the subconscious mind completely controlled him, so this person needs an adjustment to his subconscious mind which controlled him and made him a scared person because of an accident in his childhood.

From here, the person needs to be balanced and face any shortcomings he has courageously and frankly and does not hide this feeling by doing other things to make up for it.

Hitler had some sexual deficiencies, so in order to prove his manhood and leadership, he turned towards war and blood until Eva Brown, whom he adored and loved, came, but his old life and his subconscious mind completely controlled him and made him unable to change with his new love. If Eva came early, Hitler's life might have changed.

You must know that your life and the preconceived rulings, fear and conflict that are taking place are the result of previous accumulations, whether about childhood events or through hearing or fear of the future.

From here, you need to change your thinking and take over your subconscious mind, so if you are an introvert then go out to your community and contact with people. Try to program your subconscious mind on happiness until you have a habit that truly makes your conscious mind happy.

Do not leave yourself to be blamed for a mistake you did in the past, because if you did so, your subconscious mind will create an internal court that displays the crime and you will have to do your best to create the justifications for defending yourself. We are all human beings and we are all subject to error, but you must think positively and come out of a mistake with an intention not to do it again. This way you can use your subconscious mind to control the conscious one.

You must heal your subconscious mind by depending on positive thinking and believing that happiness is at the door of every human being. We are the ones who open for it to enter our lives so that we make ourselves happy or repel it, and we make ourselves miserable.

Happiness is not bought from outside, it is a seed inside you, you have to make it grow every day through positive energy and the law of internal attraction, which says that you must attract everything that makes you happy and expel everything that makes you sad, including thoughts.

Chapter 3
The power of subconscious mind

The subconscious mind in another concept is several elements that make up a someone's personality, and a person may be aware of some of these elements, while some others remain completely out of his awareness.

Intellectual schools differ in determining this concept categorically, except that an agreed upon definition of subconscious mind is a repository of tests deposited in the depth of mind resulting from psychological repression, and these tests are not related to memory. The subconscious contains behavioral stimuli, which is also the seat of emotional and sexual instinctive energy, in addition to many pent-up experiences.

Secrets of the power of the subconscious

- *Spontaneous behavior*

Many people believe that spontaneous behaviors are a product of the environment and life that a person has lived in, or perhaps things that he encounters in daily life, so he does it without any thinking, but the truth that many people are ignorant of is that the subconscious is responsible for these behaviors; Like going to eat immediately after feeling hungry, or drinking water immediately after feeling thirsty without thinking about it, and the power of the subconscious is not limited to making decisions on the biological level, but goes beyond it to make people obey it without the slightest thinking.

- *Positive or negative thinking*

Despite many attempts by many people to think positively, those attempts quickly fail, and this is due to the fact that this thinking, whether negative or positive, does not result from the conscious mind, but rather it is a feeling emanating from the subconscious mind that stores positive or negative feelings, and this subconscious mind is responsible for making decisions in the process of thinking, whether positively or negatively, and to overcome this matter a person must do the actions he loves; Like practicing some hobbies that make him happy in an attempt to give the subconscious a storehouse of positive experiences, which in turn is reflected in his daily thoughts and behavior.

- *Memory*

Advice was recently directed to the student to study immediately before bed, because this action activates the subconscious mind, the first responsible for save everything that the person sees, hears or reads, it stores the memories of pleasant and unpleasant moments.

So, the immediate reactions come directly from the subconscious mind because it extracts similar situations stored in it that a person has been exposed to in previous periods, so the immediate human reaction is based on the nature of those situations stored in the subconscious mind.

- *Law of communication or attraction*

This law may seem somewhat complicated, but it is summarized in the following form, when the subconscious mind sees that a person is going through a positive period, it directly stimulates the conscious mind in order to induce it to act according to the positive feeling stored in it.

Some may see that this matter is more intuitive, but in reality the subconscious is like a central computer that stores information, and through that stored information it has the ability to control the rest of the devices, and from here the individual's behavior towards things positively or negatively, including work; Since the subconscious knows that it is a good or bad idea, it controls the human decision to apply for a job or ignore it.

- *I'm the best*

These magical words are recommended by psychiatrists to frequently repeat it, so that the individual gains a lot of strength and self-confidence and his actions are changed into the best.

These positive phrases are the key to accessing and controlling the subconscious mind, and changing the way people solve things by harnessing the power of this mind to continuously reach success and positive feelings, provided that the statements that show the positives are repeated in every action you commit to implement.

Believe that you will succeed and be the best and keep saying it, this is the only way your desired goals will be reached, which will further motivate enthusiasm to do business in the fullest manner without delaying it.

In the end, it should be remembered that the power of the subconscious mind is the controlling of the conscious mind of man, and therefore he is in control of all behaviors issued by man, whether positive or negative, and that this subconscious mind possesses boundless power through which a person can direct his life towards better or worse.

Chapter 4
The rules of subconscious mind

The work of the subconscious is activated during sleep; If a person dreamed of a serious dream or message of warning about a specific subject, this indicates the warning of the subconscious mind to him, because the subconscious mind realizes the details of an individual's life.

To know how the subconscious mind works and how to use it, it is necessary to know and follow its laws. The subconscious has some laws that every person who wants to change himself must have sufficient knowledge of; Where the scientists reached these laws and some people applied them in their scientific and practical lives, namely:

- *Equal Thinking Law*

This law means that the things that a person thinks make him see other things that are exactly the same.

- *Attraction Law*

The Law of Attraction states that a person is like a magnet. He attracts people and events commensurate with the way he thinks, by invisible electromagnetic waves present in his subconscious mind. One of the most dangerous laws is the law of attraction. This is because human energy does not know any distances or times. For example, if a person thinks a lot about a person who is far away from him, then his energy will reach that person and then return to him.

It happens that a person often remembers another person and is surprised by seeing him or meeting him after a short period of time.

- *Replacement Law*

In order for a person to change a certain idea, he must use the law of replacement, which means that if a person wants to acquire a new habit or to replace a negative idea with a positive idea he must repeat a skill a lot in order to make it a habit for him and that it be embedded in his subconscious mind.

The following example will clarify that to you: If a person spoke to another person and said " you are bad" and repeated it, he by that sent him negative vibrations and energy that can make him behave in a negative way, he has planted bad thoughts in him. The person must always repeat positive thoughts in front of others and in front of himself to avoid bad behavior.

- *Reflection Law*

This law means that the outside world affects the inner world of a person. When a person directs a good word to another person, it will affect his soul and lead to a similar nice reaction, the other person will respond with good words and style.

- *Focus Law*

This law means that what a person focuses on will occur, and that anything that is focused on will affect the one's judgment on things, and thus the effect will be transferred to his feelings and thoughts, so if you focus on sadness and the things that make you unhappy, you will become unhappy, and so also with happiness, if you focus on the things that make you happy, you will become happy.

The focus law means that anything that exists in the mind of the inner human is the result of his behavior. So, if a person thinks about something, he must do it continuously until this thing is implanted in his subconscious mind, then it becomes a habit and a permanent behavior or experience.

- *Expectation law*

It means that what a person expects for himself will happen, just as a person's expectation of what will happen will contribute greatly to his success, only if what he expects relates to success.

The law of expectation is one of the most powerful laws. This is because anything that a person expects will lead to the sending of vibrations containing energy returning to him again carrying the same thinking that he expected. For example, if a person went to take an exam and expected that he would not know the answer, then what he expected would happen and he would not really know the answer.

- *Control Law*

This law means that a person must seek reasons, and if a person does not seek reasons, he will not reach what he wants no matter what he has of knowledge, energy and mental ability; Rather, he must put his knowledge and ability into practice so it becomes a path to his happiness rather than his misery.

- *Accumulation law*

This law states that anything a person thinks more than once and in the same manner will accumulate in his subconscious mind; Whoever thinks that he is ill and thinks about it a lot and for a long time, this will accumulate in his subconscious mind and he will actually get sick.

- *Customs Law*

This law follows the accumulation law. Since what accumulates in the subconscious mind day by day will turn into a permanent habit, it is worth mentioning that it is easy for a person to acquire a certain habit but it is difficult to get rid of it, unless he uses the laws of the subconscious mind to dispose of it in the same way as acquiring it.

- *Relaxation law*

The work of the subconscious mind happens only at times of calm and relaxation, the best example of this is that in the individual's daily life and when he is in a hurry and wants to remember a certain thing, he will not be able to remember because of the speed of thoughts or the turmoil that occurs, he must calm down to remember or find what he wants.

Therefore, the subconscious mind is the reference to all events that happen for a person, and by teaching and training it with good ideas and thoughts, individuals' lives will change, their confidence in themselves will increase, their accomplishments will increase in all aspects of life.

One must avoid thinking about bad and negative things, and always think about the positives that will please them.

Chapter 5
How to use subconscious mind to achieve your goals

Scientists are the most believing people in the power of the subconscious mind and its importance in their lives. Many scholars rely on it to gain insight and to reach their great accomplishments in the modern world. Many scientists have also relied on the strength of their subconscious mind to find facts and solutions to many of their scientific problems.

Here are some instructions to deal with the subconscious mind according to the recommendations of scientists:

- Attention and focus on the conscious mind to solve a problem directs the subconscious to collect all the important information in order to present it to the conscious mind to take the appropriate decision to solve the problem.

- The conscious mind depends on logical thinking in solving all problems, but sometimes you need some out of the box solutions to solve them, whether from others or the world around you. If you cannot find a logical solution, seek the help of your subconscious mind before bed and you will find an answer soon. Command your subconscious mind! It will follow.

- Perhaps you do not get the desired answer quickly during the same night. Continue to transfer it to your subconscious mind during the day and continue until the solution comes.

- Sometimes the answer is delayed because you feel that it is difficult to find a solution or you need a longer time to get the solution. But the subconscious does not know any boundaries of time or space, always trust that it has the right solution.

- Imagination and mental image with strong belief and continuity in demand are the keys to see the desired goal achieved, only then you will know the amazing power of the subconscious.

- The subconscious is your databank for memories from your childhood to the moment as it records all your experiences throughout your life, so choose your memories as much as you can.

- The subconscious mind helps many archaeologists and historians to imagine the past and what life was like in ancient times.

- If you are trying to get something, think confidently and faithfully before bed that it will happen to handle it into your subconscious mind, and you will get the perfect way to do it.

- Your subconscious mind respects the law of action and reaction. The more correct the data and ideas are, and the more correct the responses you get.

- Guidance comes as a feeling, and inner knowledge, it is an increasingly powerful drive when you know what you want to know. It is an internal feeling that touches the topic, so follow it.

Programming the subconscious before bed

Sleep is not only those hours that we spend far away from those around us believing that we are relieved from the burdens of the day and relax our mind from the continuous work.

It is that period that allows the subconscious to work diligently and to achieve your goals. What you dream, start with while you sleep, and always be sure that it will be achieved with certainty. The subconscious is never resting, as it is in a state of constant work.

Sleep is the best way to solve those problems that are difficult for the conscious mind to solve, so you need to share it to your subconscious mind to find the optimal solution.

How to achieve sleep miracles

You can program your subconscious mind to help you wake up at the exact time that you set for yourself before bed and you will see the miracle. Also, the subconscious mind does all the vital functions of the body so forgive yourself and others before bed as this helps your body to heal and get rid of many diseases.

The solutions and directions that you need to achieve your goal or even warnings are sent to you during sleep in the form of a dream or body signals through some "waves of healing" so you wake up actively and happily. The subconscious can give you happiness, health, confidence, and peace during sleep to face all the daily life problems ahead of you.

To get away from anxiety, depression, insomnia, mental disorder, and weak memory, you need to sleep for eight hours a day to get good physical and mental health, as insomnia causes a mental breakdown. Sleep helps you to be spiritually charged, thus you get vitality and happiness.

The subconscious can sacrifice anything in return for the desired sleep, so you find many who miss sleep, the subconscious resort to taking some naps even while driving.

Chapter 6
Control your subconscious mind

The stock of the subconscious depends on the behaviors that a person receives and learns from other people, so he acquires his basic personality from these things that the subconscious stores.

The subconscious passes states of inactivity and states of activity as well, and its activity and inactivity depend on the person himself, as he responds to any positive or negative thoughts directed to it, noteworthy; That the subconscious works without stopping, during awakening and during sleep, and it controls the state of high morale or low spirits. So, once you learn to control your subconscious mind, you will control your life.

Control methods in the subconscious

- *Inject the subconscious with ideas*

This method is accomplished by passing the ideas that we wish to achieve, from the conscious mind, directly to the subconscious, by adopting a specific idea, and being completely immersed in thinking about it, or through daydreams. This method is achieved by quiet thinking of what we really want to do, and we will note that this thing will be done exactly as you want.

Example: When you convince yourself that the exam is very easy, and that you will score a full mark, and that all words about the difficulty that accompany the subject are just nonsense, you will notice that you will really pass the difficulty and will achieve excellence with ease.

- *Seeking knowledge*

If we want to program the subconscious about what we want, we must first provide it with logical scientific ideas, which follow according to a deliberate scientific method, and away from illusion and useless imagination.

These ideas are gained by meditation, so that we form a specific image of the thing that we want to achieve, and we dwell on meditation on how to achieve it.

- *Imagine*

Imagination is one of the easiest ways to program the subconscious and control it by formulating an idea and bringing imagination around it that it has become a realistic and tangible thing. This method must be carried out with calm, relaxation, deep and slow breathing, then drowning in imagination.

- *Thanks*

When we have satisfied souls, the subconscious mind becomes programmed to accept things with great spaciousness. Thanksgiving lasts blessings, and this is a great way to program the subconscious, to thank, and to be patient, feel comfortable and feel safe, and expel negative thoughts.

- *Method of discussion and argumentation*

This method is carried out, by presenting negative thoughts and events to discussion, and reaching the conclusion that they are ideas that come from wrong beliefs; For example, when we convince a patient that his illness is not serious, that he will recover, and that treatment opportunities are guaranteed, the subconscious mind will receive these ideas, and send them to the body, so that the disease is better resisted , morale becomes very high; because positivity is high, it is half the treatment.

Important tips for controlling the subconscious

- Empirical methods must be used to program the subconscious and to engineer its ideas in a positive way

- Think about the beautiful things, that they will happen, and believe happiness in everything

- The heart also has a great role in controlling the subconscious mind, by supplying ideas of love and a sense of happiness from the heart to the mind

- Imagination and the formation of mental images benefit the subconscious more than words

- Imagine what you want to achieve continuously, and most likely it will come true

- Avoiding permanent complaining about things; because it focuses on the problem, not the solution

- Getting closer to optimistic friends who have a cheerful life ahead

Conclusion

Thank you again for purchasing and reading this book!

I hope this book was able to help you to find your way to your goals, as we helped you to discover the second half of your mind.

The next step is to use it in the best possible way that can guarantee you success.

Now write positive messages on a sheet, choose the five most important messages you want to achieve in the near future, "I am a strong person," "I am a social person," "I love mixing with people," "I can refrain from smoking soon," "I have a strong memory," etc.

Keep the paper in a prominent place or write on a notebook that always accompanies you. Read the letters frequently, consider each letter and understand it well.

Work on each message individually, start with the first message, read it over and over again, make your feeling strong with it, imagine yourself having it done and, be careful about what you say to yourself and beware not to get back to one of the negative messages.

Absolutely trust your abilities. Repeat the messages until they are realized, move to the following messages, and move from one success to another.

Finally, if you enjoyed this book, then I'd like to ask you for a favor, would you be kind enough to leave a review for this book on Amazon? It'd be greatly appreciated!

Thank you and good luck in your adventure towards your subconscious mind!

BOOKS BY THIS AUTHOR

Best Ways to Invest Money During COVID-19: Make Money at Home

There are many things we can do during the pandemic and the most productive of all is to invest it wisely. Check out this book for some tips and guidance.

Best Ways to Invest in Gold For Beginners: Quick Guide for Learning and Investing in Gold. (BONUS: 14 Ways to Establish Real Gold from Fake Gold and more!)

Gold has kept a great value for thousands of years, and until this day it still occupies this high position, due to its properties that make it at the forefront of precious metals.

As it still retains its value throughout the ages, and the belief that is embedded in people's minds is that gold is the only way to pass and conserve wealth from one generation to another.

In times of political and economic tension as well as natural disasters, investors resort to buying gold as a safe haven in the markets and as a store of value, and it is also used as a hedge against high inflation. If you want gold to be part of your investment portfolio, you can choose from several investment options in gold, each of which has different investment characteristics. In this book, we offer many ways to invest in gold, tips to make the greatest possible start and the guide by which you can avoid fraud. We hope that we could help you, best of luck!

The Adventures of Sephas (Simple Bedtime Stories for Kids: Quick Read and Illustrations Included): The Boy who Speaks 100 Languages and Helps Many People All over the World

Sephas is a gifted young boy who has a talent to speak many languages. Check out his adventures on this first part of this book series.

How to Say No to Yourself: Conquering Intermittent Fasting 101- The #1 Complete Guide for Beginners & Busy People (Bonus: No-Stress 30-Day Simple Plan, Meal Preparations, Cookbook and more!)

Intermittent fasting is currently one of the most popular health and fitness trends in the world. It will teach you the unique process of following alternative fasting and feeding cycles.

This book contains proven steps and strategies on how to intermittently fast for weight loss and also examines the concept of clean nutrition.

By reading it, you will learn practical and proven arts and practices that, if followed religiously, will create a young, vibrant, exuberant, radiant and totally different being.

Do you have to lose weight? Are you trying to adapt to that new outfit for the summer? But you don't want to fall in love with those diets and lose weight with the quick tricks of the past, you need something that really stands the test of time. Much more than a diet, you need a change in lifestyle. This is exactly what the 30 day intermittent fasting challenge offers. Intermittent fasting can restart and restore the body, helping to put metabolic processes back on track. Fasting teaches your body to burn fat instead of complex carbohydrates.

With your body poised and ready to burn fat for fuel, stubborn fatty deposits like your belly, arms and legs will evaporate quickly! It may sound too good to be true, but only by regulating the body through a dedicated and consistent fasting regimen - this is truly possible! This book provides you with the knowledge, background, and recipes to successfully perform your intermittent fasting regime over the course of 30 days.

In this book you will get:
Why fast?
What is intermittent fasting?
Intermittent fasting and your hormones
Intermittent fasting and weight loss
Eat Healthily
The Keto diet
Autophagy and intermittent fasting
Pagan's diet
Intermittent fasting methods
Intermediate fasting benefits
Dangers of intermittent fasting
Intermittent fasting programs

And, in essence, everything you need to learn how to apply the practice of intermittent fasting to your life program to reap immense intrinsic benefits and thus become a healthier, happier, better and, yes, richer being.

Made in the USA
Las Vegas, NV
29 April 2024

89282147R00018